MW00396890

Mel Bay Presents Stefan Grossman's Guitar Workshop Audio Series

Classic Ragtime Guitar

taught by
Stefan Grossman
Duck Baker
Leo Wijnkamp Jr.

CONTENTS

1 2 3 4 5 6 7 8 9 0

© 2001 BY MEL BAY PUBLICATIONS, INC., PACIFIC, MO 63069.
ALL RIGHTS RESERVED. INTERNATIONAL COPYRIGHT SECURED. B.M.I. MADE AND PRINTED IN U.S.A.
No part of this publication may be reproduced in whole or in part, or stored in a retrieval system, or transmitted in any form
or by any means, electronic, mechanical, photocopy, recording, or otherwise, without written permission of the publisher.

Visit us on the Web at www.melbay.com — E-mail us at email@melbay.com

CLASSIC RAGTIME GUITAR

by Duck Baker

Ragtime is in many ways the quintessential American music. It arrived at the turn of the century with many transitions, notably the discovery of the means to record sound, and the determination of Afro-Americans of genius to be appreciated as artists. Two factors more important to the development of 20th Century music would be hard to imagine, but the evolution of Celtic influenced, plantation-type melodies syncopated over an independent bass line with an insistent back-beat and rich tonal harmonizations might fill the order. The music we call ragtime represents not only a moment of great anticipation (as the advent of jazz was on hand) but also of fulfillment. There are, perhaps, 200 classic ragtime pieces that represent a corpus of extraordinary beauty some of the most straightforward, melodious and out-and-out joyful music that there ever was. Beneath that bubbling, free-running joy are depths of sadness that seem to contain foreknowledge of the hand that fate had in store for the music and its practitioners. Perhaps it is the nature of that fate, as much as the ultimately irrepressible good humor of ragtime, that makes me think of it as so American. It does seem that our treatment of artists and art are particularly shameful, but what is more interesting is how much great art, especially music and literature, America has given the world.

It should be made clear that ragtime was not a music that sounded completely different than what came before it, the way later forms of jazz were to do. Some 19th Century banjo compositions would be called minstrel show music today but bear all the characteristics of ragtime: from syncopation to the structure of strung-together repeated melodies. These 'minstrel' virtuosi were white musicians, such as Dan Emmett, Stephen Foster and other pop-songwriters of the day, who were influenced by black folk music. By the end of the century, black musicians were playing a kind of music that had descended from these banjo pieces, usually as background music in bars or bordellos. Though straightlaced Victorian society did not (at least officially) know about it, ragtime had spread over much of the country by the mid-1890s. There was a whole subclass of itinerant black pianists who were guaranteed employment in houses of ill-repute anywhere they wanted to go, but it was right in America's heartland that the development reached critical mass in the person of Scott Joplin of Sedalia Missouri.

Joplin's classical training is one thing that made his approach to music flexible enough to push it into more elaborate harmonic schemes than was usual. It would be a mistake to think that ragtime was not already a fairly evolved music at the time, and a greater mistake to assume that Joplin's background accounted for his abilities as a composer. It does seem fair to regard Joplin as the most important of the ragtime composers and a man who utilized every musical idea he was familiar with. In 1898, John Stark of St. Louis published Joplin's Maple Leaf Rag and the ragtime boom was born. *Maple Leaf Rag* sold over a million copies of sheet music. One wonders how sales of the music of modern hit tunes compare with that figure!

It was not long before all kinds of garbage was being cranked out by Tin Pan Alley under the guise of 'ragtime' to cash in on Maple Leaf Rag's popularity. (This probably took the same length of time as did the first Beatles imitations.) In the wave of watered-down hack-work and the usurpation of the name 'ragtime' (which had a short, obscure history to start with) the general public never had much of an idea of what ragtime really was. After a few years, they stopped caring. Listeners preferred to jump on the bandwagon of that new fad, 'jass,' with the same shallowness and fickleness that always characterize mass fads.

John Stark - an atypical exemplar for publishers - genuinely believed in the music he put out, and did his best to put real ragtime on the market. Joplin, along with two other gifted ragtime composers, James Scott and Joe Lamb, composed numerous rags of real beauty over the first ten or twenty years of the century. Unfortunately, public interest dwindled and eventually dried up.

Despite ragtime's untimely end, things went well for the first decade or so. Joplin relocated to St. Louis, then accompanied by Stark he went to New York. There, his doubly tragic role was acted out - as an artist longing to be taken 'seriously' and as a black man craving acceptance on a human level. This notion is not just liberal sentimentalizing. It is clear that the ragtime composers, like singers of spirituals, had hopes that their music might make white people accept them. I find this fact too sad to comment on, but would point out that not too many blues or even jazz musicians thought in such terms... they generally played their music for their own folk. Joplin's last years were devoted to working on an opera called Treemonisha, which really did not deserve much more than the oblivion it met before being unearthed in the 1970s. Scott Joplin died a broken man in 1917.

For years, ragtime was remembered as pizza-parlor piano-pounding or tenor banjo-flailing (minstrel banjos were the 5-string variety) complete with striped shirts, straw hats, follow the bouncing ball sing-along films, etc. There were a few keepers of the flame, like Rudi Blesh, who wrote *They All Played Ragtime* (for years the only book on the subject), and pianist Max Morath, who at one point even got ragtime on television.

In the early 1970s, a pianist named Joshua Rifkin made a recording of Joplin's music for the classical record label, *Nonesuch*. Rifkin's touch was definitely more classical than hard-hitters like Morath or even Scott Joplin or James Scott, but his understanding and feeling for the music were profound. For some serendipitous reason, Rifkin's recording caught on.

Ragtime had another boom. Pianists who sounded like they had not heard of Joe Lamb a couple of years earlier were recording his works. Gunther Schuller unearthed some charming small-band arrangements of Joplin rags and recorded them as The Red Back Book. Someone in Hollywood decided these lovely band arrangements would be the perfect soundtrack for the Paul Newman-Robert Redford feature, The Sting. Scott Joplin's name became familiar and his tunes wellknown over 50 years after his death. Then, in fairly short order, the fad passed and ragtime was once again territory for specialists, though of course nowhere near the utter obscurity it had been. In fact, I heard a dreadful muzak version of *The Entertainer* in a supermarket just the other day.

Coincidental to the ragtime revival was the coming of age of a generation of fingerpicking guitarists. In ragtime, they found a music that was vastly challenging, great fun to play, and one that adapted well to the instrument. These were, for the most part, players who had taken up the guitar during the '60s folk revival and learned how to fingerpick Elizabeth Cotten or Mississippi John Hurt tunes and were looking for more demanding material. Ragtime more than filled the bill - even 'easy' guitar ragtime is a workout.

The music itself really needs no introduction by now, so without further ado, ladies and gentleman, here is a collection of three guitar lessons featuring four arrangements for fingerstyle guitar of classic rags taught by three teachers.

Enjoy the music and have fun,.
Duck Baker

EXPLANATION OF THE TAB SYSTEM

"…Learning from listening is unquestionably the best way, the only way that suits this kind of music. You are setting the notes down for a record of what happened, a record that can be studied, preserved and so on, a necessary and useful companion to the recordings of the actual sounds. I keep thinking of this as I transcribe; if you could do it, it would be good to have a legend across each page reading : 'Listen to the record if you want to learn the song.'"

Hally Wood (taken from the Publisher's Foreword to the *New Lost City Ramblers Songbook*.)

Copyright © 1965 Oak Publications
All rights reserved. Used by permission.

These words are most suitable for introducing the tablature system, for tablature is just a guide and should be used in conjunction with the recordings. Tablature is not like music notation, however the combination of tab and music in an arrangement forms a complete language. Used together with the original recordings they give a total picture of the music.

The tab system does not attempt to show rhythms or accents. These can be found on the music or heard in the recordings. Music notation tackles these articulations to a degree, but the overall sensations, the feel and the soul of music cannot be wholly captured on the written page. In the words of the great Sufi Hazrat Inayat Khan: "…The traditional ancient songs of India composed by great Masters have been handed down from father to son. The way music is taught is different from the Western way. It is not always written, but is taught by imitation. The teacher sings and the pupil imitates and the intricacies and subtleties are learned by imitation."

This is the theme I've tried to interpolate into the tablature. Tablature is the roadmap and you are the driver. Now to the tab:

Each space indicates a string. The top space represents the first string, second space the second string, etc. A zero means an open string, a number in the space indicates the fretted position, for instance a 1 in a space indicates the first fret of that string.

In the diagram below the zero is on the second string and indicates the open second string is played. The 1 is placed on the third string and signifies the first fret of the third string. Likewise, the 4 is in the fourth space and indicates the fourth fret of the fourth string.

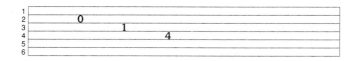

Generally for fingerpicking styles you will be playing the thumb, index and middle fingers of your picking hand. To indicate the picking finger in tab the stems go up and line up down from the numbers.

A. A stem down means that your thumb strikes the note.
B. If a stem is up, your index or middle finger strikes the note. The choice of finger is left up to you, as your fingers will dictate what is most comfortable, especially when playing a song up to tempo!

C. The diagram below shows an open sixth string played with the thumb followed by the second fret of the third string played with the index or middle finger:

In most cases the thumb will play an alternating bass pattern, usually on the bass strings. The index and middle fingers play melodic notes on the first, second and third strings. Please remember, this is not a rule; there are many exceptions.

In fingerpicking there are two "picking" styles: Regular picking and "pinching" two notes together. A pinch is shown in the tab by a line connecting two notes. A variation of this can also be two treble notes pinched with a bass note. Follow the examples below from left to right:

1) The open sixth string is played with the thumb.
2) The first fret of the sixth string is pinched together with the third fret on the third string. The sixth string is played with the thumb, the third string with the index finger.
3) The thumb strikes the third fret of the fourth string.
4) The first fret/sixth string is played with the thumb; it's pinched with two notes in the treble. The index and middle fingers strike the first fret/first string and the third fret/second string.
5) The next note is the index finger hitting the first fret/second string.
6) Lastly, the bass note is played with the thumb on the third fret/fourth string.

There are certain places in blues and contemporary guitar that call for the use of either strumming techniques or accented bass notes. The tab illustrates these as follows:

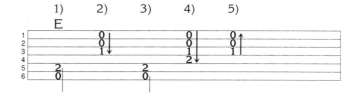

1) The thumb hits the open sixth string and the second fret on the fifth string should also sound. For example, play an E chord. Now strike the open string and vary the force of your attack. Try hitting it hard enough so that the fifth string vibrates as well. This technique is very important for developing a full sound and the right alternating bass sound.

2) Next the arrow notation indicates a brush and the arrowhead indicates the direction of the brush.

    A. If the arrowhead is pointed down, the hand brushes up towards the sixth string.
    B. If pointed up, the hand brushes down towards the first string.
    C. The number of strings to be played by the brush is shown by the length of the arrows. For example, this arrow shows a brush up toward the sixth string, but indicates to strike only the first, second and third strings.
    D. The brush can be done with your whole hand, index finger or middle and ring finger. Let comfort plus a full and "right" sound guide your choice.

3) The third set of notes again shows the sixth string/open bass note played with the thumb and being struck hard enough to make the fifth string/second fretted position sound.

4) Once more an arrow pointed downward indicates a brush up. This example forms an E chord and the brush up includes the first, second, third and fourth strings.

5) The last set of notes has an arrow pointed upward, indicating a brush downward striking the first, second, and third strings.

Here are several special effects that are also symbolized in tablature:

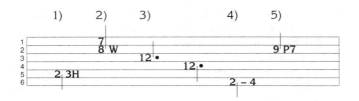

1) HAMMER-ON: Designated by an "H" which is placed after the stem on the fret to be hammered. In the example above, fret the second fret/fifth string and pick it with your thumb. Then "hammer-on" (hit hard) the third fret/fifth string, i.e. fret the third fret/fifth string. This is an all-in-one, continuous motion which will produce two notes rapidly with one picking finger strike.

2) WHAM: Designated by a "W." In the example the eighth fret/second string is "whammed" and played with the seventh fret/first string. Both notes are played together with your index and middle fingers respectively. The whammed note is "stretched." We do this by literally bending the note up. We can "wham" the note up a half tone, full tone, etc.

3) HARMONICS: Symbolized by a dot (•). To play a harmonic: gently lay your finger directly above the indicated fret (don't press down!) The two notes in the example are both harmonics. The first on the twelfth fret/third string is played with the index/middle finger, while the second note—twelfth fret/fourth string—is played with the thumb.

4) SLIDE: Shown with a dash (–). Play the second fret/sixth string and then slide up to the fourth fret of the sixth string. This is a continuous movement: the string is struck once with your thumb.

5) PULL-OFF: "P" designates a "pull-off." Fret both the seventh and ninth frets on the second string. Play the ninth fret with your index/middle finger and then quickly remove it in the same stroke, leaving the seventh fret/second string. Pull-offs are generally in a downward direction.

6) In certain cases other specific symbols are added to the tab, for instance:
    A. For ARTIFICIAL HARMONICS an "X" is placed after the fretted position.
    B. For SNAPPING a note an indication may be given with a symbol or the written word.

Many times these special techniques are combined, for instance putting a pull-off and a hammer-on together. Coordination of your fretting and picking hands will be complex initially, but the end results are exciting and fun to play.

PICKING HAND POSITION FOR FINGERPICKING STYLES: The Classical and Flamenco schools have strict right-hand rules, however for this style of acoustic fingerpicking there are NO RULES, only suggestions. Your right hand position should be dictated by comfort, however in observation of many well-known fingerpickers I found one hand position similarity—they all tend to rest their little finger and/or ring finger on the face of the guitar. This seems to help their balance for accenting notes and control of the guitar. Experiment with this position: it may feel uncomfortable at first. I ask my students to perfect this position and then compare the sound to when their finger(s) were not placed on the face of the guitar. They usually find the sound is greatly improved when some contact is kept with the guitar face.

MUSIC NOTATION: We have somewhat adapted the music notation in that this also shows whether the note is picked with your thumb or index/middle fingers. The stems of the music notes correspond to the direction of the tab stems. I hope this will make the music notation clearer to fingerpicking guitarists.

I hope you will feel at home and comfortable with the tablature and musical notations. Remember, these are only road maps indicating where and how you should place your fingers. The playing and musical interpretation is up to you.

INTERLUDE

10

B² (Performance Variation)

17

D.S. al ⊕   ⊕¹
Continue at ⊕¹

18

SILVER SWAN

Drop D Tuning: DADGBE

Attributed to Scott Joplin and arranged for guitar by Ton Van Bergeyk © 1988 Shining Shadows Music (BMI)   All Rights Reserved. Used With Permission

HILARITY RAG

Tuning: DGDGBE

Composed by James Scott, 1910 and arranged for guitar by Leo Wijnkamp Jr. © 2001 Shining Shadows Music (BMI) All Rights Reserved. Used With Permission

28

CD Track Listings

The audio lessons in this series were originally recorded in the 1970s. They were initially released on audio cassettes. We have gone back to our master tapes to get the best possible sound for this new CD edition. The complete contents of the original recordings have been maintained but certain references to albums that are no longer available or information that is out of date have been edited out.

These lessons originally came with different print material. These were handwritten and in some cases offered only tab transcriptions. The lessons have now been typeset in tab/music. As a result some spoken references on the CDs regarding page numbers or a position of a line or phrase on a page may differ slightly from the written tab/music in this new edition. We have annotated as carefully and exactly as possible what each track on the CDs present. Please use these track descriptions as your reference guide.

Lesson One - taught by Stefan Grossman

Track 1: Performance of *The Entertainer*
Track 2: Introduction to *The Entertainer*
Track 3: Tuning to Dropped D tuning (D A D G B E)
Track 4: Teaching of introduction
Track 5: Plays slowly introduction
Track 6: Teaching of first bar of *Section A*
Track 7: Plays slowly first bar of Section A
Track 8: Teaching of second to fourth bars of *Section A*
Track 9: Plays slowly second to fourth bars of *Section A*
Track 10: Teaching of fourth to sixth bars of *Section A*
Track 11: Plays slowly from first bar to sixth bars of *Section A*
Track 12: Teaching of sixth to twelfth bars of *Section A*
Track 13: Plays slowly from fourth to twelfth bars of *Section A*
Track 14: Teaching of end of twelfth bar to end of *Section A*
Track 15: Plays slowly from end of twelfth bar to end of *Section A*
Track 16: Teaching of first and second endings of *Section A*
Track 17: Plays slowly *Section A*
Track 18: Teaching of first two bars of *Section B*
Track 19: Plays slowly first two bars of *Section B*
Track 20: Teaching of third bar to end of *Section B*
Track 21: Teaching of *Interlude*
Track 22: Teaching of first and second ends of *Section B*
Track 23: Plays slowly *Section B*

Track 24: Teaching of first two bars of *Section C*
Track 25: Plays slowly first two bars of *Section C*
Track 26: Teaching of third and fourth bars of *Section C*
Track 27: Plays slowly third and fourth bars of *Section C*
Track 28: Teaching from fourth to sixth bars of *Section C*
Track 29: Plays slowly fourth to sixth bars of *Section C*
Track 30: Teaching of seventh and eighth bars of *Section C*
Track 31: Plays slowly from seventh to thirteenth bars of *Section C*
Track 32: Teaching of fourteenth bar to end of *Section C*
Track 33: Teaching of first and second endings of *Section C*
Track 34: Plays slowly *Section C*
Track 35: Teaching of first two bars of *Section D*
Track 36: Plays slowly first two bars of *Section D*
Track 37: Teaching from third to sixth bars of *Section D*
Track 38: Plays slowly fifth and sixth bars of *Section D*
Track 39: Teaching from seventh to eighth bars of *Section D*
Track 40: Plays slowly from thirteenth bar to ending of *Section D*
Track 41: Plays slowly *Section D*
Track 42: Introduction to Scott Joplin performing *The Entertainer*
Track 43: Scott Joplin performing *The Entertainer*
Track 44: Closing thoughts on *The Entertainer*
Track 45: Jim McLellan performs *The Entertainer*

Lesson Two taught by Duck Baker and Stefan Grossman

Track 1: Performance of *Maple Leaf Rag* on piano
Track 2: Duck Baker plays *Maple Leaf Rag*
Track 3: Introduction to *Maple Leaf Rag*
Track 4: Tuning
Track 5: Teaching of first two bars of *Introduction*
Track 6: Plays slowly first two bars of *Introduction*
Track 7: Teaching of third and fourth bars of *Introduction*
Track 8: Plays slowly third and fourth bars of *Introduction*
Track 9: Teaching of fifth and sixth bars of *Introduction*
Track 10: Plays slowly fifth and sixth bars of *Introduction*
Track 11: Teaching of seventh and eighth bars of *Introduction*
Track 12: Plays slowly seventh and eighth bars of *Introduction*
Track 13: Teaching of first four bars of *Section A*
Track 14: Plays slowly first four bars of *Section A*
Track 15: Teaching of fifth and sixth bars of *Section A*
Track 16: Plays slowly fifth and sixth bars of *Section A*
Track 17: Teaching of seventh and eighth bars of *Section A*
Track 18: Plays slowly seventh and eighth bars of *Section A*
Track 19: Plays slowly *Section A*
Track 20: Teaching of first eight bars of *Section B*
Track 21: Plays slowly first eight bars of *Section B*
Track 22: Teaching from thirteenth bar of *Section B*
Track 23: Plays slowly from thirteenth bar of *Section B*
Track 24: Plays slowly *Section B*
Track 25: Teaching of first two bars of *Section C*
Track 26: Plays slowly first two bars of *Section C*
Track 27: Teaching of third and fourth bars of *Section C*
Track 28: Plays slowly third and fourth bars of *Section C*
Track 29: Teaching of fifth and sixth bars of *Section C*
Track 30: Plays slowly fifth and sixth bars of *Section C*

Track 31: Teaches from seventh bar to end of *Section C*
Track 32: Plays slowly *Section C*
Track 33: Teaching of first two bars of *Section D*
Track 34: Plays slowly first two bars of *Section D*
Track 35: Teaching of third and fourth bars of *Section D*
Track 36: Plays slowly first four bars of *Section D*
Track 37: Teaching of fifth to eighth bars of *Section D*
Track 38: Plays slowlu fifth to eighth bars of *Section D*
Track 39: Teaching of bars nine to sixteen of *Section D*
Track 40: Plays slowly *Section D*
Track 41: Performance of *Silver Swan Rag*
Track 42: Introduction to *Silver Swan Rag*
Track 43: Tuning (Dropped D tuning D A D G B D)
Track 44: Plays slowly *Introduction*
Track 45: Teaching of *Introduction*
Track 46: Plays slowly *Introduction*
Track 47: Teaching of first two bars of *Section A*
Track 48: Plays slowly first two bars and continues teaching to fourth bar of *Section A*
Track 49: Plays slowly first four bars and continues teaching to eighth bar of *Section A*
Track 50: Plays slowly first eight bars and continues teaching to end of *Section A*
Track 51: Teaching of first four bars of *Section B*
Track 52: Plays slowly first four bars and continues teaching from fifth to eighth bars of *Section B*
Track 53: Plays slowly first eight bars and continues teaching to end of *Section B*
Track 54: Plays slowly *Section B*

Lesson Three taught by Leo Wijnkamp Jr.

Track 1: Performance of *Hilarity Rag*
Track 2: Introduction to *Hilarity Rag*
Track 3: Tuning to D G D G B E
Track 4: Teaching of first four bars of *Section A*
Track 5: Plays slowly first four bars of *Section A*
Track 6: Discussion of bass figure in third and fourth bars and continues teaching from fourth to twelfth bars of *Section A*
Track 7: Plays slowly from eighth to twelfth bar of *Section A*
Track 8: Teaching from twelfth bar to end of *Section A*
Track 9: Plays slowly *Section A*
Track 10: Teaching of first four bars of *Section B*
Track 11: Plays slowly first four bars of *Section B*
Track 12: Teaching of fifth to eight bars of *Section B*
Track 13: Plays slowly fifth to eighth bars of *Section B*
Track 14: Plays slowly from ninth to twelfth bars of *Section B*
Track 15: Teaching from thirteenth bar to end of *Section B*
Track 16: Plays slowly *Section B*
Track 17: Teaching of repeat ending of *Section B* and discussion of structure of arrangement
Track 18: Plays slowly *Section A*

Track 19: Plays slowly *Section B*
Track 20: Teaching of first four bars of *Section C*
Track 21: Plays slowly first four bars of *Section C*
Track 22: Teaching from fifth to eighth bars of *Section C*
Track 23: Plays slowly ninth to twelfth bars of *Section C*
Track 24: Teaching from thirteenth bar to end of *Section C*
Track 25: Plays slowly thirteenth to sixteenth bars of *Section C*
Track 26: *Plays slowly Section C*
Track 27: Teaching of first four bars of *Section D*
Track 28: Plays slowly first four bars of *Section D*
Track 29: Teaching from fifth to eighth bars of *Section D*
Track 30: Plays slowly ninth to twelfth bars of *Section D*
Track 31: Teaching from thirteenth bar to end of *Section D*
Track 32: Plays slowly *Section D*
Track 33: Discussion on structure of sections and end tags of *Hilarity Rag*
Track 34: Closing thoughts on *Hilarity Rag*
Track 35: Plays slowly all four sections (without repeats) of *Hilarity Rag*
Track 36: Introduction to *Sycamore Rag*
Track 37: Performance of *Sycamore Rag*